REALITY TV TITANS

GETTING GRITTY WITH
Mike Rowe

Jill C. Wheeler

**Checkerboard
Library**

An Imprint of Abdo Publishing
abdopublishing.com

abdopublishing.com

Published by Abdo Publishing, a division of ABDO, PO Box 398166, Minneapolis, Minnesota 55439.
Copyright © 2016 by Abdo Consulting Group, Inc. International copyrights reserved in all countries.
No part of this book may be reproduced in any form without written permission from the publisher.
Checkerboard Library™ is a trademark and logo of Abdo Publishing.

Printed in the United States of America, North Mankato, Minnesota

062015
092015

THIS BOOK CONTAINS
RECYCLED MATERIALS

Design: Jen Schoeller, Mighty Media, Inc.
Production: Mighty Media, Inc.
Series Editor: Liz Salzmann
Cover Photos: Getty Images, front cover; AP Images, back cover
Interior Photos: Alamy, pp. 13, 15, 17, 23; AP Images, p. 27; Corbis, p. 21; Mighty Media, Inc., p. 19;
Seth Poppel/Yearbook Library, pp. 8, 9; Shutterstock, pp. 3, 5, 7, 11, 12, 25, 29

Library of Congress Cataloging-in-Publication Data

Wheeler, Jill C., 1964-
  Getting gritty with Mike Rowe / Jill C. Wheeler.
    pages cm. -- (Reality TV titans)
  Includes index.
  ISBN 978-1-62403-818-1
1. Rowe, Mike, 1962- 2. Television personalities--United States--Biography. 3. Actors--United States
--Biography. I. Title.
  PN1992.4.R75W64 2015
  791.4502'8092--dc23
  [B]

2015010221

CONTENTS

Mike Rowe

Mike Rowe is the host of *Dirty Jobs*. He is known as the "dirtiest man on television." Rowe has made a career out of trying jobs that most people don't want to do. By doing this, he has brought recognition to the people who do these jobs every day.

Rowe believes skilled labor is no less important than office work. He believes people should be more connected to the trades. Trades are jobs that require manual skill. These jobs make important things such as plumbing, electricity, agriculture, and transportation possible.

Rowe didn't start out as a labor champion. His first television job was being a host on a home shopping network. Since then, he has had a successful career as a voice talent, actor, and producer. Rowe is at ease whether in front of a camera or as a voice-over **narrator**. His humor, warmth, and easygoing style have won him many fans. *Dirty Jobs* is just as popular and successful as Rowe. It has been nominated for four Emmy Awards.

Mike Rowe at the Primetime Emmy Awards in 2008

Early Inspiration

Michael Gregory Rowe was born March 18, 1962, in Baltimore, Maryland. He was John and Peggy Rowe's first child. Mike's parents were both teachers. Mike has two younger brothers, Phil and Scott.

The Rowes did not have much money. But they taught their children that wealth and material things were not important. They said pizza delivery was for children who were not lucky enough to get home-cooked meals. And vacations were for people who didn't have a farm where they could play.

The Rowe brothers did have a farm to play on. They lived next to their grandparents on a farm outside Baltimore. Rowe describes his grandfather as "a plumber, a mechanic, a mason, and a carpenter." Mostly though, Mike saw him as a magician. His grandfather left the house in the morning and worked all day solving other people's dirty problems. Seeing this, Mike grew up with great respect for physical labor. And his grandfather eventually became Mike's inspiration for *Dirty Jobs.*

Growing up in rural Maryland greatly influenced Mike's future career.

Finding His Voice

Mike went to Overlea High School in Baltimore. He was talented at acting and singing. This was not a surprise, as Mike's parents were also talented performers. His father appeared in more than 100 community theater plays. His mother was a singer and pianist.

Mike's senior yearbook photo

Mike's music teacher, Fred King, supported Mike's growing talent. He encouraged Mike to find jobs using his voice. Mike recorded an advertisement for a mattress store when he was still in high school.

Rowe graduated from high school in 1980. He went on to study theater at Essex Community College in Essex, Maryland. He later transferred

Mike *(left)* was in the musical *Oklahoma!* in high school.

to Towson State University in Towson, Maryland. There, he studied English, communications, speech, and music.

Rowe graduated from Towson State in 1985. To support himself, he worked as a salesman for a computer company. Yet he continued to follow his interest in the arts. He performed in community theater productions and did voice-over projects.

From Opera to TV

Rowe continued to work and participate in the arts. In 1984, he decided to **audition** for the Baltimore Opera Company. He had no training in opera singing when he auditioned. However, he earned a spot in the company.

Six years later, Rowe's career took another turn. He went to a bar one day with a friend from the opera company. They were both still wearing their opera costumes. The bar's television was tuned to the QVC home shopping channel. The **bartender** told them that QVC was holding auditions in Baltimore that week.

The bartender ended up betting Rowe one hundred dollars that he would not get a **callback** if he tried out. Rowe took the bet and went in for an audition. During his performance, Rowe spent nearly eight minutes talking about a pencil. QVC hired him on the spot.

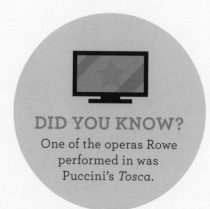

DID YOU KNOW?
One of the operas Rowe performed in was Puccini's *Tosca*.

Rowe performed at the Lyric Opera House, located near downtown Baltimore.

QVC Salesman

Rowe worked at QVC for the next three years. His job was to discuss items for sale and interest viewers in buying them. Rowe often worked in the middle of the night, when there were fewer viewers. He learned how to spend a lot of time talking about nothing.

Rowe sold more than $100 million in synthetic diamond jewelry on QVC.

Although Rowe was good at selling QVC products, the experience was not always smooth. He sometimes made fun of the show's products. Other times he said things about QVC viewers that some people found insulting.

Because of this, Rowe was fired and re-hired more than once. In 1993, he left QVC for good.

Many QVC viewers thought Rowe was a funny, entertaining salesman.

Host Extraordinaire

Rowe left QVC, but he did not leave the television industry. He had learned a lot about it during his time on QVC. He decided to use what he had learned in the next chapter of his career. Rowe got a job as the host of *Egypt Week Live* on the Discovery Channel.

Rowe's Discovery Channel job took three weeks to film. Afterward, he went on to host many other shows. They included *Your New Home, Worst Case Scenarios*, and the History Channel's *The Most*. In 2001, Rowe started hosting a talk show in San Francisco, California, called *Evening Magazine*.

While working at *Evening Magazine*, Rowe started a new feature. He called it "Somebody's Gotta Do It." During these **segments**, Rowe explored dirty jobs such as being a trash collector. These were his first experiences with doing dirty jobs on television.

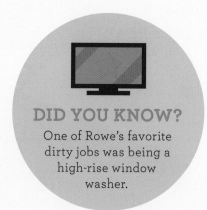

DID YOU KNOW?
One of Rowe's favorite dirty jobs was being a high-rise window washer.

Rowe on *Worst Case Scenarios*

Dirty Work

Rowe's "Somebody's Gotta Do It" **segments** became popular on *Evening Magazine*. He decided to send a copy of the feature to his contacts at the Discovery Channel. He wanted to see if he could bring the concept to a larger **audience**. The network's executives were interested. They asked Rowe to make a similar show for them.

The Discovery Channel released three **episodes** of *Dirty Jobs* in November 2003. **Critics** and viewers loved the show. Discovery Channel executives quickly made plans to turn it into a regular series.

Dirty Jobs first aired as a regular series on July 26, 2005. It featured Rowe working for people who do what are considered dirty jobs. He collected trash, worked on a pig farm, farmed algae, and inspected **sewers**. The show was a smash hit. Almost immediately, *Dirty Jobs* became the Discovery Channel's second most popular program.

DID YOU KNOW?
Rowe wrote and sang a song, "The Dirty Ditty," for the one-hundredth episode of *Dirty Jobs*.

Rowe stuck in mud working on a yak farm in Montana
is a typical *Dirty Jobs* moment!

Dirty Jobs lasted eight seasons and aired more than 160 **episodes**.
Rowe worked more than 300 jobs. Throughout the series, Rowe made
viewers laugh, **cringe,** and be altogether disgusted. His hands-on
approach to all things dirty kept viewers coming back for more.

Extreme Jobs

Rowe is often asked what is the grossest job he has ever encountered on *Dirty Jobs*. He says the grossest job was working with people who removed roadkill. The remains of animals often end up spread across the road.

Rowe has a different answer for what was the hardest job he tried on the show. In 2014, he said the hardest job he did was chipping concrete. He has also said indoor **demolition** and moving houses were exhausting.

And the absolute dirtiest job? Rowe says it was working inside Bracken Cave in Texas. The Bracken Cave is the summer home of the world's largest colony of bats. For this *Dirty Jobs* **episode**, Rowe entered the cave with a bat biologist. They checked on the 40 million bats that live there. Television could not convey just how smelly and uncomfortable that job was. Rowe felt bats brush against him. Beetles crept into his socks and bit him. Worst of all, the cave was filled with an overpowering smell of the bats' waste.

Inspired by Mike Rowe
Worm Farm

Materials

- **large plastic bottle**
- **scissors**
- **small rocks**
- **ruler**
- **sand**
- **dirt**
- **fruit or vegetable peels**
- **4 to 5 worms**
- **nylon stocking**
- **rubber band**
- **black paper**
- **tape**

1. Ask an adult for help.

2. Cut off the top of the bottle.

3. Put a layer of rocks in the bottle.

4. Add 2 inches (5 cm) of sand and 2 inches (5 cm) of dirt.

5. Repeat step 4 until the bottle is almost full. Add a few pieces of peel before the final layer of dirt. They will feed the worms.

6. Add the worms.

7. Lay a piece of stocking over the top of the bottle. Use a rubber band to hold it on.

8. Wrap the paper around the bottle. Tape the edge to make a tube. Slide it off to watch the worms. Otherwise, keep the farm covered.

9. Keep the dirt wet, but not flooded. Add more peels a couple of times a week.

Dangerous Jobs

In addition to being gross or hard, many of the jobs featured on *Dirty Jobs* can be **dangerous**. Rowe has been thrown off a horse, kicked by cows, scratched by cats, bit by an ostrich, and stung by bees. His scariest incident was when a blacksmith's furnace burned off his eyelashes.

Rowe putting himself in danger on some **episodes** is part of the reality of some jobs. His goal is to show everyone what doing those jobs is really like. Sometimes that means showing **audiences** just how dangerous they are. However, he also takes the same precautions as the people who do those jobs on a daily basis.

In 2012, Rowe's dangerous experiences on *Dirty Jobs* came to an end. The show's final episode aired that fall. But Rowe continued his television career. In 2014, he moved to CNN to host a new show with a similar focus. In *Somebody's Gotta Do It*, Rowe visits people who chose to do something unusual. These have included inventors, **entrepreneurs**, and collectors.

Rowe wears goggles and other safety equipment when necessary for protection.

Trades Activist

Rowe learned a lot from doing *Dirty Jobs*. His experiences working with people doing tough, physical jobs taught him what **blue-collar** work really means to people. He decided to use his resources to bring attention to these important fields.

In 2008, Rowe made a TED Talk about the changing face of the American blue-collar work force. Rowe spoke about the importance of these jobs to society. He has learned that America faces a shortage of people who can do them.

That same year, he also launched mikeroweWORKS. This public relations campaign and website promotes the importance of blue-collar jobs. The site encourages visitors to find jobs that they love, even if they are unusual. And the mikeroweWORKS Foundation offers **scholarships** to people who want to master the trades.

DID YOU KNOW?
Rowe signs autographs in exchange for donations to the mikeroweWORKS Foundation.

Rowe helped start the "I Make America" campaign. It works to create more manufacturing jobs.

Rowe in Washington

In 2011, Rowe went to Washington, DC. He spoke to members of the United States Senate Commerce Committee. He explained that students are not usually encouraged to learn the trades anymore. There are important jobs that not enough people are being trained to do. This is creating a gap in the skills necessary in the workforce.

Rowe talked about how attitudes about work have changed. Getting a four-year college degree is seen as the ideal path. Work in the trades is often considered to be just for those who are not suited for college. Rowe said many parents and young people today see **apprenticeships** and on-the-job-training as "**vocational** consolation prizes."

To change the way trade jobs are viewed, Rowe asked Congress to help support his work to promote skilled labor. People depend on these types of jobs every day. These jobs provide things such as transportation, shelter, and electricity. Rowe doesn't think it's right that they are often viewed as second-class jobs.

Rowe addressed the US Senate Commerce Committee in the Russell Senate Office Building.

Keeping Busy

Today, Rowe is a busy guy. In addition to hosting shows and advocacy work, he continues to work as a **narrator**. He has narrated shows such as *Deadliest Catch* and *American Chopper*. In all, Rowe estimates that he has narrated more than 1,000 hours of television programming. Rowe is also a popular public speaker. He is frequently asked to talk about his former work on *Dirty Jobs*.

Rowe's narrating and hosting work has been well received. He is popular among **critics** and fans. He has more than 200,000 followers on Twitter and more than 2 million likes on Facebook. In 2011, Rowe won the Critic's Choice TV Award for "Best Reality Host." *Forbes* magazine included Rowe on its ten most-trusted celebrities list in 2010, 2011 and 2012.

Rowe continues to earn fans and work hard. He continues to speak up for people who want to have careers in the trades. When he has spare time at home in San Francisco, Rowe enjoys reading. But for a busy and successful guy such as Rowe, there is not much spare time!

Rowe is known as a hardworking, honest man who sticks up for everyday people.

Timeline

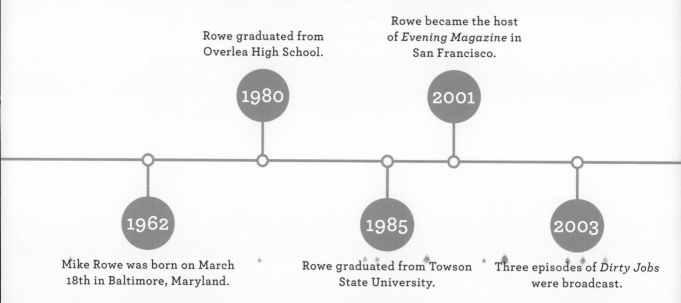

Rowe graduated from
Overlea High School.

Rowe became the host
of *Evening Magazine* in
San Francisco.

1980

2001

1962

1985

2003

Mike Rowe was born on March
18th in Baltimore, Maryland.

Rowe graduated from Towson
State University.

Three episodes of *Dirty Jobs*
were broadcast.

Mike Rowe Says

"I believe there is no
such thing as a 'bad job.'
I believe that all jobs
are opportunities."

"It's a dirty job . . .
but somebody's
gotta do it."

"Don't follow
your passion, but
always bring it
with you."

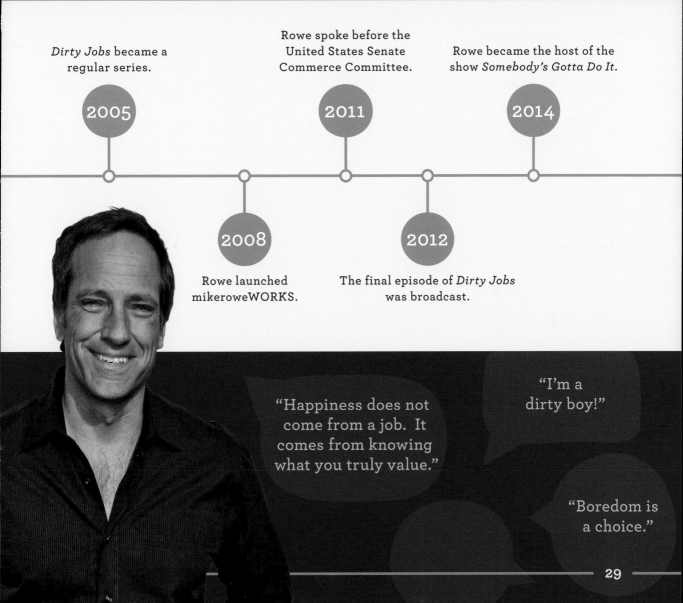

2005 — *Dirty Jobs* became a regular series.

2008 — Rowe launched mikeroweWORKS.

2011 — Rowe spoke before the United States Senate Commerce Committee.

2012 — The final episode of *Dirty Jobs* was broadcast.

2014 — Rowe became the host of the show *Somebody's Gotta Do It*.

"Happiness does not come from a job. It comes from knowing what you truly value."

"I'm a dirty boy!"

"Boredom is a choice."

Glossary

apprentice – a person who learns a trade or a craft from a skilled worker. A position as an apprentice is an apprenticeship.

audience – a group of people watching a performance.

audition – a short performance to test someone's ability.

bartender – someone whose job is to serve drinks in a bar.

blue-collar – related to jobs that don't require college degrees and usually involve physical labor.

callback – a second audition for a role in a play or other performance.

cringe – to react with fear or distaste.

critic – a professional who gives his or her opinion on art, literature, or performances.

dangerous – able or likely to cause harm or injury.

demolition – the act of tearing down or destroying something.

entrepreneur – one who organizes, manages, and accepts the risks of a business or an enterprise.

episode – one show in a television series.

narrate – to tell a story. A person who narrates is a narrator.

scholarship – money or aid given to help a student continue his or her studies.

segment – a scene on a specific topic that is part of a longer show.

sewer – an underground passage used to carry away waste.

vocational – relating to training in a skill or trade to be pursued as a career.

Websites

To learn more about Reality TV Titans, visit booklinks.abdopublishing.com. These links are routinely monitored and updated to provide the most current information available.

Index